This book belongs to

....

....

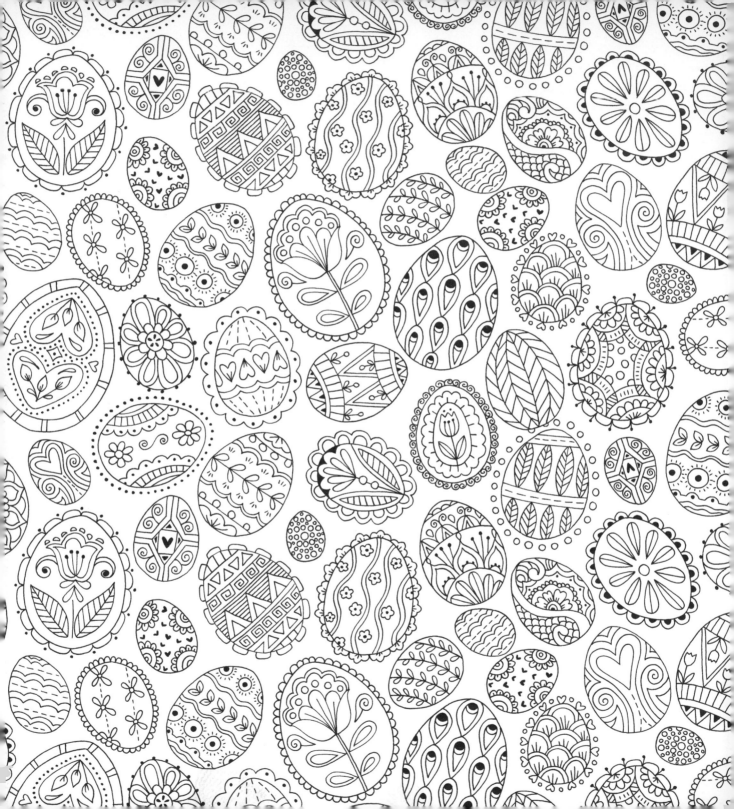

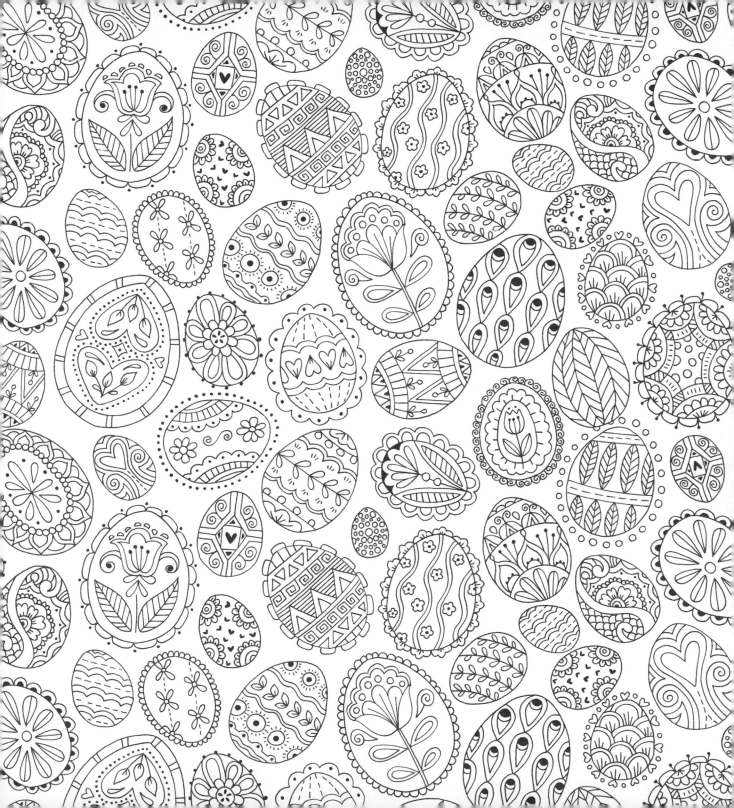

For Andy (1979–2000), with love   A.J.
For Jason (1987-2009), who always thought
I'd do art, with love   F.F.

Text by Antonia Jackson
Illustrations copyright © 2017 Felicity French
This edition copyright © 2017 Lion Hudson

The right of Felicity French to be identified as illustrator of this work has been asserted
by her in accordance with the Copyright, Designs and Patents Act 1988.

Published by Lion Books
an imprint of
Lion Hudson plc
Wilkinson House, Jordan Hill Road,
Oxford OX2 8DR, England
www.lionhudson.com/lion

ISBN 978 0 7459 7690 7

First edition 2017

A catalogue record for this book is available from the British Library

Printed and bound in Spain, December 2016, LH39

THE LION
Easter
COLOURING BOOK

Retold by Antonia Jackson
Illustrated by Felicity French

LION

Long ago in Galilee there lived a man named Jesus.
"You are all welcome in God's kingdom," he told
the crowds who gathered to listen to him.
"Even little children.
"To be a friend of God, love God with all your heart.
"And love one another. Do for others what you would
like them to do for you.
"Forgive those who are unkind to you,
and God will forgive you."

One day, Jesus and his friends left Galilee
for Jerusalem.
"We will go to the Temple in Jerusalem to
celebrate the Passover," he told them.
When the crowds saw Jesus riding into the city,
they cheered.
"Hooray for Jesus!" they cried. "Hooray for
God's chosen king."
They cut palm branches and waved them.

But Jesus hadn't said anything about
being God's chosen king.
Jesus went to the Temple, where the festival
market was in full swing.
He tipped up the stalls and chased the
stallholders away.
"This is meant to be a place to pray," he cried,
"not to make money."

The priests and the teachers who saw
this were not happy.
"That Jesus makes trouble everywhere
he goes!" they said.
"The crowds greeted him like a king,
and now he has upset the Temple.
"How can we stop him?"
Then Judas, one of Jesus' friends,
came to see the priests.
"If you pay me, I'll help you catch Jesus,"
Judas told them.

Jesus and his friends
shared the festival meal.
Jesus passed them the cup of wine
and broke a loaf of bread into pieces.
"When I am gone, share a meal like
this to remember me," he told them.
Meanwhile, Judas had slipped away.

Jesus knew Judas was going to betray him.
He took his friends to an olive grove called Gethsemane,
where he prayed to God. "Please, God, do not let me
suffer. But if it is what you want, let it be so."
Through the darkness, Jesus saw Judas coming with
soldiers holding torches. They seized Jesus and marched
him away to his enemies.

"You're a troublemaker!" the priests
told Jesus. He hadn't done anything wrong,
but the priests had made up their minds.
They took him to the Roman governor,
Pontius Pilate.
"This man is a rebel," the priests said.
"He claims to be a king.
"He must be stopped!"
Sorrowfully Pilate gave his army an order:
"Take this Jesus
and put him to death on a cross."

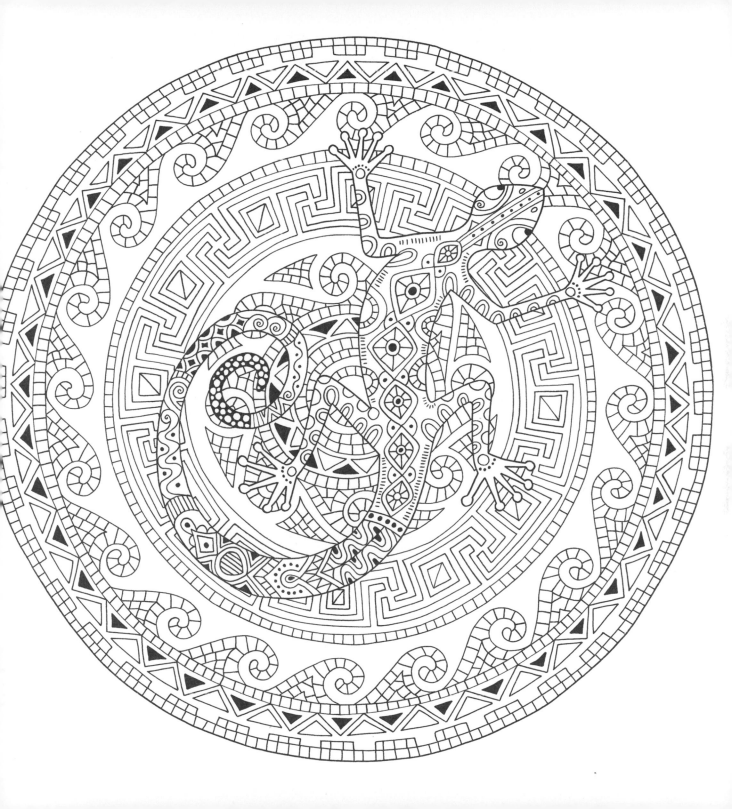

The soldiers took Jesus to a hill outside
Jerusalem and nailed him to a cross.
He said a prayer for his enemies: "Forgive them,
Father God. They don't know what they're doing."
His friends stood a little way off, watching.

Later, Jesus' friends came to take his
body down from the cross.
They laid it in a tomb and rolled the
stone door shut.
"There isn't any time for funeral customs,"
the women cried. "It's nearly sunset, when
the sabbath day of rest begins."
And they hurried away.

Early on the Sunday morning,
the women came back to the tomb.
They were astonished to find that the stone door
was open – and the tomb was empty.
They saw two angels there. "Jesus is not here,"
they said. "He is alive!"

Mary Magdalene, one of the women,
stayed weeping by the tomb.
She heard a voice ask, "Why are you crying?"
Mary turned and said, "You must be the
gardener. Have you seen Jesus?"
The man said to her, "Mary."
And then she knew – it was Jesus!

Over the next few days, Jesus
appeared to his friends.
"Soon I will leave you and go to heaven,"
he told them.
"I want you to carry on my work.
"Spread the good news I have told
you about God. Show people how
to live as God's friends.
"Go and tell everyone in the world about
God's love – the love that
will last forever."

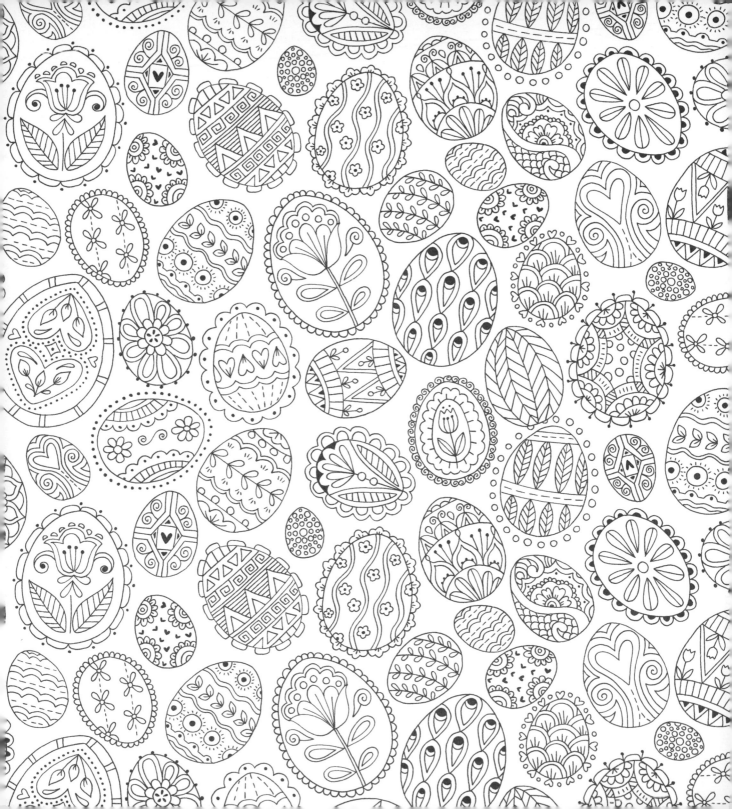

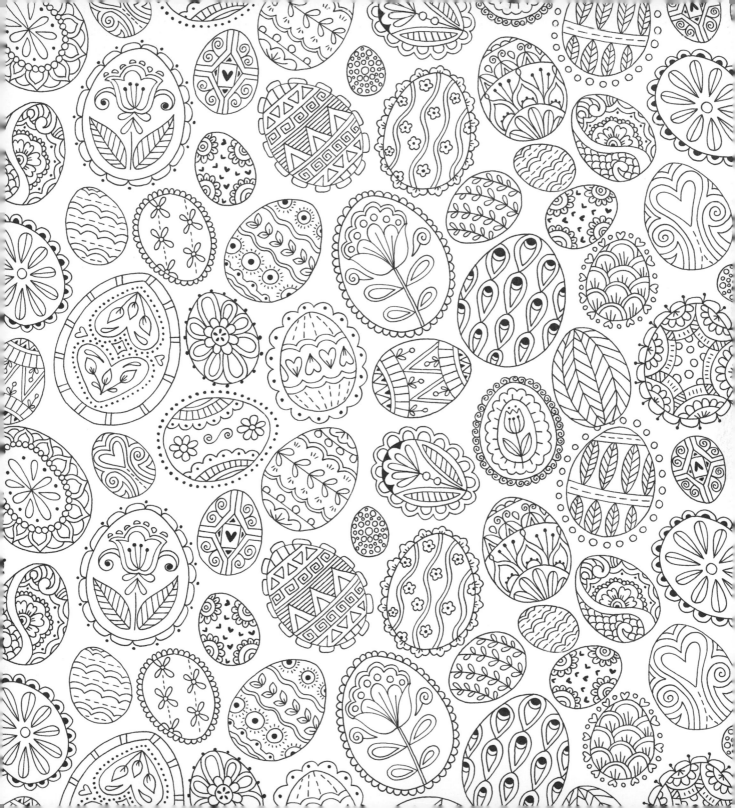

Also from Lion Books

The Lion Psalms Colouring Book   *Antonia Jackson & Felicity French*
The Lion Nativity Colouring Book   *Antonia Jackson & Felicity French*
The Lion Bible Verses Colouring Book   *Antonia Jackson & Felicity French*

Easter titles from Lion Children's Books

The Easter Story   *Antonia Jackson & Giuliano Ferri*
The Story of Easter   *Mary Joslin & Alida Massari*
Easter! Fun Things to Make and Do   *Christina Goodings*